ZWINGER PALACE
DRESDEN

TRAVEL TO LANDMARKS

ZWINGER PALACE DRESDEN

John Man
Photographs by Nicolas Sapieha

Tauris Parke Books, London

The author and photographer would like to thank Helga Schlegel for her help in the production of this book.

All photographs by Nicolas Sapieha except frontispiece and pages 14-15, 17, 18, 21, 22, 27, 48-9, 57-9, 61, 72, 75, 76, 78, 79, 80-1, 82 (top right), 98, 102-3.

Published by Tauris Parke Books
110 Gloucester Avenue, London NW1 8JA
In association with KEA Publishing Services Ltd., London

TRAVEL TO LANDMARKS

Series Editor: Judy Spours
Editorial Assistant: Elizabeth Harcourt
Designer: David Robinson
Maps by John Hewitt

British Library Cataloguing in Publication Data

Man, John
Zwinger Palace, Dresden. – (Travel to Landmarks)
1. East Germany. Dresden. Palaces. Zwinger Palace, history
I. Title II. Series
943.2142

ISBN 1-85043 177-9

Photosetting by Litho Link Ltd., Welshpool, Powys, U.K.
Colour separations by Fabbri, Milan, Italy
Printed by Fabbri, Milan, Italy

FRONTISPIECE Detail from Canaletto's view of the Zwinger Palace painted in about 1750 (see page 72).

Contents

Map of Old Dresden 6
Introduction: A Jewel in a Battered Crown 9

1. Augustus the Strong 23
   Groundplan of the Zwinger Palace 24

2. A World of Art 51
   The Mathematical-Physical Salon 65

3. Of Galleries and Paintings 73
   Friedrich August II 73
   The Old Masters Gallery 74

4. Destruction and Rebirth 101
   Survival and Renewal 114

Travellers' Information 125

Index 127

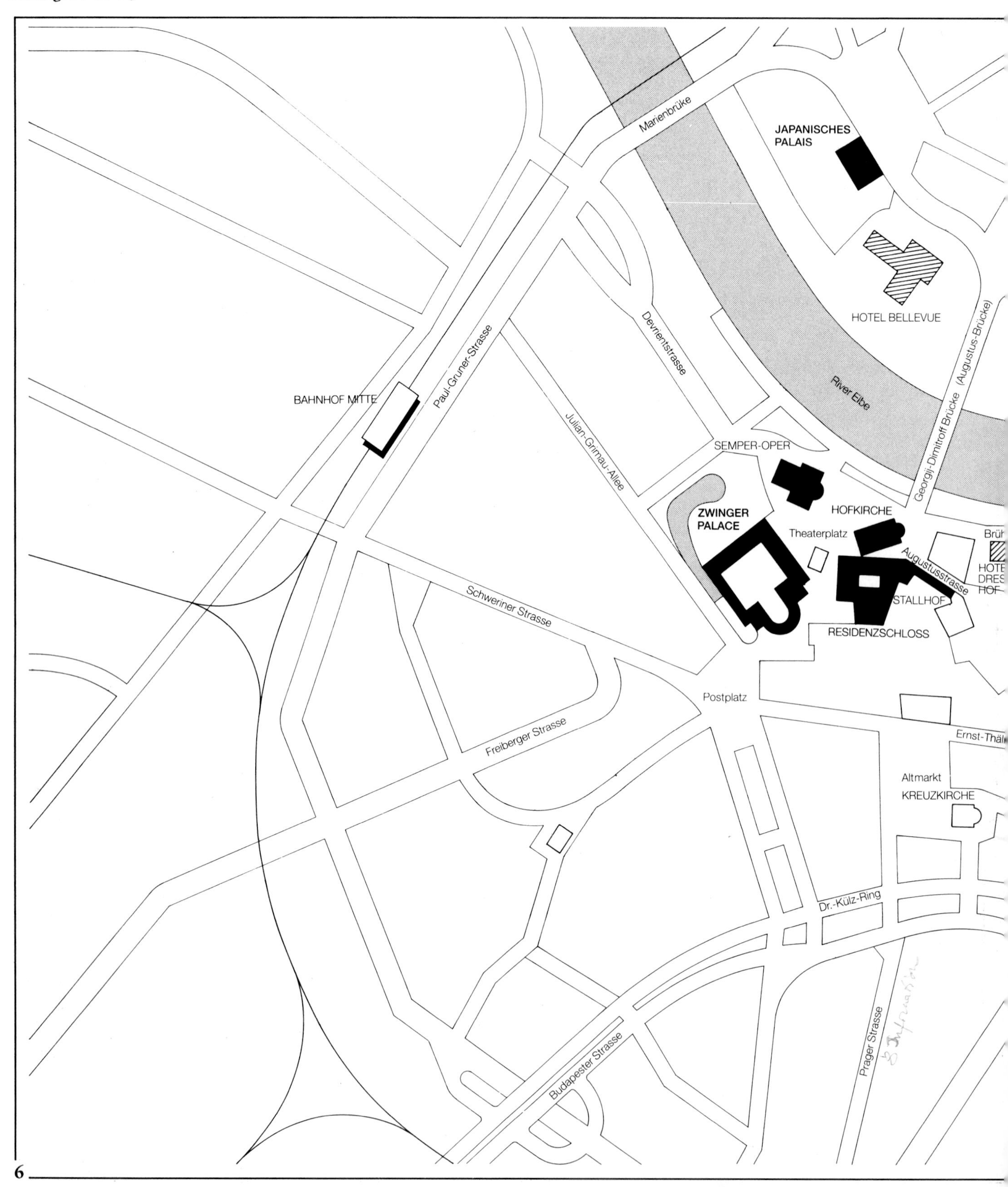

Marienbrüke
JAPANISCHES PALAIS
HOTEL BELLEVUE
Georgij-Dimitroff Brücke (Augustus-Brücke)
River Elbe
Devrientstrasse
Paul-Gruner-Strasse
BAHNHOF MITTE
Julian-Grimau-Allee
SEMPER-OPER
ZWINGER PALACE
HOFKIRCHE
Theaterplatz
Augustusstrasse
STALLHOF
RESIDENZSCHLOSS
Schweriner Strasse
Freiberger Strasse
Postplatz
Ernst-Thäl
Altmarkt
KREUZKIRCHE
Dr.-Külz-Ring
Prager Strasse
Budapester Strasse

MAP OF OLD DRESDEN

Introduction: A Jewel in a Battered Crown

The Stables, with their intricate black and white decorations, were built by Elector Christian I in the late sixteenth century to house the huge collections of arms and armour that would later be formed into the Historical Museum.

There's no denying that the approaches are beautiful, if you approach from the right direction. Dresden's outlying villages are cradled by the enfolding arms of hills that sweep the River Elbe into wide and graceful curves. The well-spaced villas and peasant cottages could, with a touch of paint, be as charming as they once were.

But as you near the centre, you see that Dresden is still a wounded city. The poorly healed scars of war show in the grim modern apartment blocks, sparsely set like weeds in a bomb site. There's nothing here to remind you that Dresden was once called 'Florence on the Elbe', with a reputation for elegance, beauty and fashion to rival any city in Europe.

Wait, though. As you come to the river, you see a historic stone bridge leading over sturdy spans to a slender church tower. You cross the bridge, moving with a current of people towards the church. Its eighteenth-century tower seems like the prow of a graceful ship, dividing the flow of people to left and right, towards buildings, streets and squares of an intimacy and beauty for which the drab surroundings are no preparation at all.

This is Dresden's heart, a family of buildings nestling together in an area only a few hundred metres across. At first, it's hard to make out what you're looking at. Ahead, the church is connected by a covered, copper-clad and tarnished footbridge to some huge place that is still in ruins. To the left, there are several classical buildings, ranged along an embankment, obviously an ancient battlement. That way, there are lanes, overarching roofs, a sense of medieval huddle. To the right, a contrast: the road swings round to a huge square dominated by a grand nineteenth-century opera house.

You stroll in that direction. To the left more ruins, more confusion, roofless walls, blackened rubble, mud, scaffolding and cranes. You are in the midst of a long and painful rebirth. Beyond the opera house, a fine classical façade. You saunter past the end of the façade. It is a section of a larger building. You glance in the main entrance, and pause. The style here is not at all classical, nor forbiddingly grand. Its stonework is ornate, intricate, delicate, all scrolls and complex curlicues. It draws you. There is a gateway, but no door. Beyond the shadows is a burst of light, inviting you to pass through.

Inside, it's like walking into an amphitheatre. The ornate stonework falls back on either side, not that you are aware of the setting for a second or two, because the space ahead is what fills your mind. It is like a huge open-air stage, seeming to invite a performance, or a pageant, or a spectacle of some kind. As you walk out among the formal paths and fountains into the broad strong light pouring down from the open sky, you see you are right. It's not a place for living in. It is a symmetrical swirl of pavilions and walls, an architectural froth of glass, stone, grass and fountains, a setting for royal revelry.

You are in the Zwinger Palace, the jewel in Dresden's battered, historic crown.

It is much more than an array of gorgeous façades. As soon as it was built 275 years ago, it became the embodiment of Dresden's greatness. Its collections of art made it a focal point for creative people from all over Europe. To the people of Dresden, it was the very symbol of their city; and its reconstruction after the horrific events of 1945 made it equally a symbol of the city's survival and rebirth.

It takes a rich, self-confident nation to provide conditions favourable for the creation of buildings like the Zwinger. Those conditions had taken 500 years to build. Saxony, the nation eventually ruled from Dresden, began its rise to wealth and influence in the twelfth century. This Saxony, by the way, has nothing to do with another pre-existing Saxony, the original homeland of the tribal Saxons, now recalled in the name of the West German state of Lower Saxony, 'lower' because it is further down the Elbe; the name was transferred in the twelfth century to lands on the upper Elbe as part of a complicated re-allocation of lands and titles.

This, the later Saxony, was fortunate. In about 1168, silver was found in the virtually uninhabited mountains on the borders of present-day Czechoslovakia, some sixty-five kilometres south of Dresden. One fifteenth-century mine, St Georg in the district of Schneeberg, yielded 20 tons of silver. Rapidly, other finds were made: gold, tin, copper and iron – the area was named the Erzgebirge (Ore Mountains) – and semi-precious stones galore: agate, serpentine, garnet, amethyst, opals, quartz, and many others. It became Germany's treasure-house. 'The Bohemian border is all tunnelled through and hollowed out,' wrote an eighteenth-century traveller. 'All ravines ring with the sound of hammer mills.'

The wealth of raw materials supported armies of craftsmen, creating every type of object: jewellery, armour, swords, cutlery, bowls, statuettes, furniture, coins, medals. Saxony's silver talers were one of

ABOVE The approaches to Dresden are as charming as ever, especially from the west, where the Elbe swings beneath the woods and vineyards of the Elbhänge hills, leaving an open flood plain that leads across to suburbs, many of whose villas survive from the eighteenth and nineteenth centuries.

BELOW The new building that surrounds Dresden's historic core is frankly drab, fulfilling Socialist East Germany's immediate post-war need for housing.

Zwinger Palace, Dresden

ABOVE LEFT The Dimitroff Bridge – previously the Augustus Bridge – leads across the Elbe to the spindly tower of the Hofkirche and the solid mass of the Residence, the former home of Saxony's Wettin dynasty. The Zwinger lies out of sight round to the right.

ABOVE RIGHT In outlying villages, wooden buildings from earlier times still survive.

BELOW Approaching the Zwinger from Opera House Square, you are confronted with a blank wall that gives no clue to the complex glory that lies within.

OVERLEAF The Zwinger's courtyard embraces visitors with arcaded galleries that seem to grow like welcoming arms from the decorated sleeves of the pavilions. The design is geometric, but because the lines are broken by curves, it never seems severe. The central space, once open for festivities, is now broken by swirling formal arrays of gardens, pools and fountains. In this view, the Wall Pavilion is on the right, the Mathematical-Physical Salon on the left. Courtesy Archiv Für Kunst und Geschichte, Berlin.

Europe's leading currencies. Small Saxon towns built cathedrals and halls that were the envy of great cities elsewhere in Europe.

The treasure flowed, of course, under the control of Saxony's dukes and princes, who were united under the authority of the ruling family, the Wettins. The Wettins came from Meissen, a few kilometres north of Dresden. With their wealth secured by control of the silver trade, they became rulers of Saxony, then known as Saxe-Wittenberg, in the fifteenth century. They inherited considerable political influence, for the ruler was an Elector, being one of the seven German princes who elected the German Emperor, the nominal head of German lands. By ancient tradition, this confused patchwork of several hundred territories was also supposedly the remnants of the Roman Empire; and since these lands were now Christian, the Emperor was crowned by the Pope, thus becoming head of what was still known anachronistically as the Holy Roman Empire.

The then capital, Wittenberg, was the cradle of religious reformation, for it was here in 1517, on the door of All Saints' Church, that Martin Luther began the Reformation by nailing up his condemnation of the Catholic practice of selling forgiveness of sins. This practice, among others, had made the Church extremely wealthy, and an important market for works of art. In the religious struggle that followed, Saxony became a leading Lutheran, or Protestant, power. The Church suffered and the State prospered. So did its people: Church lands – over 300 estates, along with their houses and riches – were confiscated and much of the wealth put into public education. Unluckily for posterity, however, anti-Catholicism fuelled iconoclasm. Thousands of art-objects, commissioned by the Church or with religious subjects, were destroyed.

Not long afterwards, the Wettin family divided, one branch inheriting lands largely outside present-day Saxony. Eventually from its dynastic maze sprang the Saxe-Coburg line, which in its turn produced Albert, who married Queen Victoria. The other line, the Albertines, kept Saxony. They also kept the office of Elector. By the mid-sixteenth century, under Elector Augustus I, Saxony became the richest German state, under the most powerful family after the imperial rulers, the Habsburgs. Augustus was a careful king, more ambitious for peace and consolidation than territorial gain. He strengthened Dresden's royal castle, the Residence (Residenzschloß), and two parallel lines of solid

fortifications anchoring the Residence and its surroundings to the Elbe.

This chancy progression from inconsequence to absolutism is recalled by a 100-metre panorama of Saxon rulers made of 20,000 Meissen tiles which were set into the wall of the Residence at the turn of the century. It is an impressive array, reminiscent of those diagrams in anthropology textbooks showing a noble *homo sapiens* emerging from stooped and blinkered ape-dom. The labels are there to help you with charming nineteenth-century nicknames: Konrad the Great, Albrecht the Proud, Heinrich the Enlightened, various Friedrichs – the Bitten (his mother bit him on the cheek to mark him with a reminder of some evil deed done to the family), the Serious, the Pugnacious, the Soft-Hearted – and on through George the Bearded and Henry the Pious to Augustus, and beyond.

It was quite in character for the prudent Augustus to see the value in the royal collection of art that had survived the Reformation. In 1560, these pieces, several hundred of them, together with hundreds of new ones, were assembled together in an Art Chamber (Kunstkammer). In addition, there was an arms and armour collection so extensive that it already had its own curator. These formed the foundation for all Dresden's later art collections.

Not that Augustus's aims were aesthetic. Now that spiritual values were out of fashion, the purpose behind the decision was practical and political. Containing mainly tools and scientific instruments, the collection displayed power, increased prestige and provided models of excellence to be emulated by goldsmiths, gunsmiths, armourers, clock-makers, potters and sculptors. There were some notable pieces of art, like portraits by Albrecht Dürer and the Cranachs, father and son, but there is a sturdy realism about even these that betrays their original, practical purpose. One drawing by Dürer of a rhinoceros records in anatomical detail an animal that in 1515 was shipped from India to Lisbon; as the poor creature was being unloaded, it fell into the harbour and drowned. Portraits were treasured as an exact representation of looks rather than works of art. Beauty is almost an incidental attribute, the consequence not of an aesthete's design but of a craftsman's skill. A royal travelling box, for instance, with a pine frame veneered in oak and ebony, now strikes visitors as a glorious work of art. But its contents reveal its original practical purpose – 250 objects used in hunting, surgery, chemistry, painting, gardening and lathe-turning, all

This 1943 view shows the Zwinger and its surroundings in their final form before war-time bombing shattered them. The Wall Pavilion is at the far left-hand end, the main entrance on the right. The gardens and fountains had been finished only fifteen years before, completing original designs left unfinished to accommodate festivities. Semper's Opera House dominates its own square, while the Hofkirche – its tower obscured by that of the Residence – guards the Augustus Bridge over the Elbe. From the air, it is easy to see how the dark mass of the Semper gallery slams the door on the original concept: to have the Zwinger opening out into the Opera House Square, bracketing an open space that would run down to the river. Courtesy Sächsische Landesbibliothek, Abt Deutsche Fotothek, Dresden.

1514
L C

Duke Henry the Pious and his wife Katharina of Mecklenburg ruled Saxony in the sixteenth century, when they were painted by Lucas Cranach the Elder, the court painter to the Wettins in Wittenberg. The photographic accuracy of the faces reveals that a principal official purpose of the portraits was practical: to record a likeness. The gorgeous clothing displays Wettin majesty, and the wreaths of carnations in the couple's headdresses recall their recent marriage (in 1512, two years before the painting was done). But there is more to the pictures than that. There are the first full-length portraits painted in Europe, a style apparently suggested by the shape of side-panels on altars, which had proved suitable for full-length views of saints. It is a constraining framework, and the poses seem ungainly. Yet character still comes through in Henry's aggressive stance and the jaunty set of his wreath, a contrast to Katharina's stodginess. Courtesy Archiv Für Kunst und Geschichte, Berlin.

the activities considered important for the well-educated all-rounder.

In addition to the Art Chamber, Augustus built a Secret Depository (Geheime Verwahrung), in which were stored cash reserves, state documents and the most precious objects. The vault, in the ground floor of the Residence, was built for total security. It had walls two metres thick, heavy bars on the windows, and a vaulted roof strong enough to withstand the collapse of the building above it, should it burn down. The only entrance was concealed within the walls and led directly up winding stairs to a living room in the palace above. The vault was painted with the dominant colour of the Saxon coat of arms, green. In years to come the room itself, and its collection, would become known as the Green Vault (Grünes Gewölbe).

Over the next eighty years, the royal collection continued to grow. In 1606, an inventory of the arms and armour alone covered 1500 pages. In the late sixteenth century, the Elector, Christian I, decided that this particular collection needed its own store. Among other things, he inherited over 100 suits of tournament armour that were used in the jousts put on for the entertainment of the court. To house the prize pieces of the collection and to provide a better setting for the courtly entertainments they were used for, he built a whole new wing to the Residence, a stable yard overlooked by an arcaded gallery. Now known as the Johanneum, it is the building that displays the tiled panorama of Saxon kings on its outside wall. It is well restored, with its black-and-white decorations as crisp as when they were first made.

The Thirty Years War of 1618–48, a continuation of religious and political strife in a series of interlocking wars, devastated much of central Europe, but Saxony emerged from the welter of violence and shifting alliances with its economic foundations – and its collections of armour, paintings and artefacts – still intact.

By the 1690s, therefore, Saxony could count itself lucky. It was a self-contained, secure, stable, wealthy state, already with an international reputation for the skill of its craftsmen and the brilliance of its collections. Its wealth and strength were attributes vital to its survival, existing as it did within a chequerboard of rival kingdoms and empires, all of them engaged in complex power-struggles that involved dynastic marriages, diplomacy, bluster and all too often brutally destructive wars. To the east lay Poland, a vast country eight times the size of Saxony, made notoriously unstable by its competing nobles. Further east still was Russia, where Peter the Great was attempting to impose his own version of *perestroika*, reforming the administration, economy and international relations by seeking contact with the West. To the south lay the Catholic Habsburg empire of Austro-Hungary, which included Protestant Czechoslovakia. To the north Protestant Sweden, in an expansionist phase that had antagonized neighbouring Prussia, Denmark, Poland and Russia. It would take not just strength and wealth but also considerable guile to ensure the preservation and extension of Saxony's interests.

At this point, there came to the throne a king who was almost man enough for the job: Friedrich August I, better known as Augustus 'the Strong'. He intended to make Dresden the most glittering cultural centre of northern Europe, with a masterpiece – the Zwinger – at its centre.

The Wettins made a point of acquiring Dürer's work, for he was among the most famous of sixteenth-century artists as the man who brought Renaissance styles to Germany. This portrait is of Bernhard van Reesen, the son of a distinguished Danzig merchant. Courtesy Sächsische Landesbibliothek, Abt Deutsche Fotothek, Dresden.